Children's Authors

Maurice Sendak

Mae Woods
ABDO Publishing Company

visit us at
www.abdopub.com

Published by ABDO Publishing Company, 4940 Viking Drive, Suite 622, Edina, Minnesota 55435. Copyright © 2000 by Abdo Consulting Group, Inc., Pentagon Tower, P.O. Box 36036, Minneapolis, Minnesota 55435 USA. International copyrights reserved in all countries. No part of this book may be reproduced in any form without written permission from the publisher.

Published 2000
Printed in the United States of America.
Second printing 2002

Photos: AP/Wide World, Corbis
Editors: Bob Italia, Tamara L. Britton, Kate A. Furlong
Art Direction: Pat Laurel

Library of Congress Cataloging-in-Publication Data

Woods, Mae.
   Maurice Sendak / Mae Woods.
     p. cm. -- (Children's authors)
   Includes bibliographical references (p.) and index.
   Summary: Presents the life of the artist and author known primarily for his award-winning illustrated children's books.
    ISBN 1-57765-112-X
    1. Sendak, Maurice--Juvenile literature. 2. Authors, American--20th century--Biography--Juvenile literature. 3. Illustrators--United States--Biography--Juvenile literature. 4. Children's stories--Authorship--Juvenile literature. [1. Sendak, Maurice. 2. Authors, American. 3. Illustrators.] I. Title.

PS3569.E6 Z95 2000
741.6'42'092--dc21
[B]   99-089169

Contents

Early Life

*M*aurice Sendak was born in Brooklyn, New York, on June 10, 1928. His parents, Philip and Sarah, were from Poland. Maurice had an older sister, Natalie, and an older brother, Jack.

Each night their father told them a bedtime story. He invented exciting, imaginative tales. Some of his stories were scary. Sometimes, the story was long and lasted many nights. Maurice had many sleepless nights, but he could hardly wait for each new episode.

Maurice was a **frail** child who was often home sick. He didn't like school. He was not good at sports. So, he spent long days gazing out the window watching people. He drew pictures of what he saw.

Brooklyn, New York, where Maurice Sendak was born

Books

*N*atalie gave Maurice his first book. It was *The Prince and the Pauper* by Mark Twain. The book smelled good and had a pretty cover. Maurice became interested in books and how they were made.

His father bought a set of books by Mark Twain. Each volume had a green cover with a gold, raised **profile** of the author on the spine. Maurice remembers that he enjoyed rubbing his finger along Twain's big nose. Since then, he has believed that books should be beautiful objects. The look and feel of the cover and the pages are as important as the contents.

Jack wrote stories and read them to the family. Maurice drew pictures on pieces of cardboard and held them up to accompany Jack's words. Their parents encouraged their efforts.

Mark Twain wrote many popular children's classics such as **The Adventures of Tom Sawyer** *and* **The Adventures of Huckleberry Finn.**

7

Early Jobs

While at Lafayette High School, Maurice created a comic strip for the school paper, *Lafayette News.* It was called "Pinky Carrd." A teacher admired Maurice's work and asked him to illustrate a science textbook called *Atomics for the Millions.*

These illustrations were Maurice's first **published** artwork. Later, he got a job at All-American Comics filling in background details for "Mutt and Jeff" comics. At age 19, Maurice was a published illustrator.

Maurice graduated from high school in 1947. He worked for awhile at Timely Service Company building window displays. He began taking classes at the Art Students League. He went to museums to study paintings and spent hours at his window **sketching** kids playing on the street.

Maurice and his brother Jack decided they wanted to go into business. They built six models of **mechanical** wooden toys. Jack **designed** the movable parts. Maurice carved and painted them. They took their toys to New York's largest toy store, F.A.O. Schwarz. The store manager said the toys were beautiful but would be difficult to manufacture. Then, he offered Maurice a job designing window displays.

Designing a window display at an F.A.O. Schwarz toy store in New York City

Maurice's Big Break

While he was working at F.A.O. Schwarz, Maurice loved to visit the book department. There, he met Frances Chrystie. Frances bought books from **publishers** for F.A.O. Schwarz to sell.

Frances discovered that Maurice was interested in illustration. She introduced him to Ursula Nordstrom. Ursula was a children's book **editor** at Harper and Brothers, one of New York's biggest publishing houses.

Maurice showed Ursula his **sketchbook**. She admired his work and hired him to illustrate Marcel Ayme's *The Wonderful Farm* in 1951. In 1952, Maurice illustrated Ruth Krauss's *A Hole Is to Dig*. Both books were successful. Maurice was finally able to support himself illustrating books.

Ursula continued to give Maurice illustrating jobs. She also encouraged him to write stories of his own. In 1956, Maurice wrote his first book, *Kenny's Window*. He also drew the illustrations. *Very Far Away*, Maurice's second book, was **published** in 1957.

Sendak started out illustrating children's books. Soon, he was working on other projects such as this American Express ad.

Rosie

*T*here was an imaginative little girl in Maurice's Brooklyn neighborhood named Rosie. She entertained the other kids with **elaborate** stories she made up and performed on the street. Maurice watched her from a window and **sketched** many drawings of her when he was an art student.

Maurice decided to write a book about her. *The Sign on Rosie's Door* was published in 1960. His readers enjoyed Rosie, too.

Maurice's next work was a set of four small books called The Nutshell Library. The books were *Alligators All Around*, *Chicken Soup with Rice*, *One Was Johnny*, and *Pierre*. The books were only 2.5 inches (6 cm) wide and 4 inches (10 cm) high, just right for little hands to hold.

Rosie was so popular that Maurice created an animated television special about her called "Really Rosie Starring the

Nutshell Kids." In this show, Rosie's playmates are the characters from the Nutshell Library books: Alligator, Johnny, Pierre, and the boy from *Chicken Soup with Rice*. Each character performs his own story.

Carole King **composed** the music for the cartoon and sang the part of Rosie. The TV show was also released on videotape. In 1981, Maurice created a stage musical, *Really Rosie*, based on the TV show.

Carole King

The Best Book Yet

When Maurice started to write *Where the Wild Things Are*, the story was about a boy's adventure with wild horses. But Maurice wasn't very good at drawing horses. So he decided to write about wild things instead. But what would the wild things look like? Maurice had an idea.

When he was young, his mother's relatives often came to visit. He thought they were horrible. "My mother always cooked for them," Maurice remembers, "and, as I saw it, they were eating up all our food. We had to wear good clothes . . . they cooed over you and pinched your cheeks. Or they'd lean way over with their bad teeth and hairy noses, and say something threatening like 'You're so cute I could eat you up.' And I knew if my mother didn't hurry up with the cooking, they probably would."

So, Maurice's aunts and uncles became the models for the wild things in *Where the Wild Things Are*.

Some grown-ups thought the wild things were too scary for children. But kids loved them. Almost one million hard cover and two million paperback copies of *Where the Wild Things Are* have been sold.

Where the Wild Things Are won the 1964 **Caldecott Medal**. British **composer** Oliver Knussen made the book into an opera.

Where the Wild Things Are *has been published in 14 languages.*

A Difficult Time

*I*n 1967, Maurice was in England. One day, he felt sick. When he went to the doctor, he found out he had suffered a heart attack.

While he was getting well, he learned his dog Jennie was sick, too. He went home to America to get well and take care of Jennie. But Jennie died.

During this time, Maurice's mother had cancer. Soon, she died, too. Maurice was sad to lose both his mom and his best friend, Jennie.

Maurice wrote a book which captured Jennie's spirit called *Higglety Pigglety Pop*. It tells the story of a dog who has everything yet believes "there must be more to life than having everything."

The dog leaves her comfortable home to see what the world has to offer. In the end, the clever dog becomes the star of the World Mother Goose Theatre and enjoys **applause** and laughter every day.

Maurice dedicated *In the Night Kitchen* to his parents. It is the story of a boy who dreams that he is being baked into a cake by three bakers. He escapes in an airplane that he makes out of dough.

The book has many things from Maurice's childhood in it. "I wanted to do a book that would say good-bye to New York and say good-bye to my parents, and tell a little bit about the narrow squeak I had just been through." But Maurice's luck was about to change.

In 1970, Maurice was awarded the Hans Christian Andersen Illustrator's Medal. This award is the world's greatest honor for excellence in children's book illustration. He was the first American to win the award.

Maurice's work was famous all over the world. In 1983, he won the Laura Ingalls Wilder award for his lasting contribution to children's **literature**.

Theater

*M*aurice was a successful author and illustrator. But he had always wanted to work in the theater. So, in 1980, he wrote the words for an opera version of *Where the Wild Things Are.* He **designed** the sets, too.

Classical music has always been important to him. He listens to music while he works. His favorite **composer** is Mozart. In his book *Outside Over There*, he actually drew a picture of Mozart writing the opera *The Magic Flute*.

In 1980, Sendak designed the sets for a production of this opera in Houston, Texas. He also designed sets for a production of *The Nutcracker Suite* ballet in Seattle, Washington.

After Sendak's success in the theater, actor Robert Redford invited him to be **artistic director** of the Sundance Children's Theater in 1988. Two years later, Sendak founded his own theater company in New York. He named it The Night Kitchen after one of his most popular books.

Maurice Sendak discusses the witch's house that he designed for the set of PBS's production of "Hansel and Gretel."

Maurice Sendak Today

*M*aurice Sendak lives in Ridgefield, Connecticut, with his dog Runge. He often helps young artists by offering encouragement and recommending their work. He understands how difficult it can be to complete a work of art.

Maurice Sendak has illustrated over 80 books. He drew the pictures for the Little Bear series, *Mrs. Piggle-Wiggle's Farm*, and a version of *Grimm's Fairy Tales*.

Maurice continues to illustrate other authors' books. He also continues to write and illustrate his own books. In 1993, Maurice wrote a book about being homeless. It is called *We Are All in the Dumps with Jack and Guy*. In 1996, he won the National Medal of Arts for his contribution to art and culture. In 1999, he illustrated his friend James Marshall's **posthumous** book *Swine Lake*.

Maurice Sendak writes books that make some grown-ups uncomfortable. But kids understand his books. They have made him one of the world's best-known authors.

Maurice Sendak (right) and Sony Corporation's Michael Swinney celebrate the opening of San Francisco's Sony Metreon entertainment complex, which contains a **Where the Wild Things Are** *interactive play space.*

Glossary

applause - the clapping of hands after a show or concert to show enjoyment.

artistic director - the person who supervises the artists and technicians in the production of a play.

Caldecott Medal - an award given by the American Library Association to the author of the year's best picture book. Books that are runners-up are called Caldecott Honor Books.

compose - to write music. A person who writes music is called a composer.

design - to plan and arrange something with artistic skill. A person who designs things is called a designer.

editor - a person who is in charge of preparing a work for publication.

elaborate - to create something very detailed with great care.

frail - without strength and easily sick.

literature - writings that have to do with a particular subject. Children's literature is books written for children.

mechanical - operated by a machine.

posthumous - a work that is published after the author's death.

profile - a picture of someone taken from the side; a side view.

published - produced and packaged for sale to the public. A publisher is a person who produces printed materials for sale. A business that publishes books is called a publishing house.

sketch - a quick drawing. Sketches are usually drawn on a pad of paper called a sketchbook.

Internet Sites

1996 National Medal of Arts
http://arts.endow.gov/artform/lit/sendak.html
This page from the National Endowment for the Arts discusses Maurice Sendak's work and his 1996 National Medal of Arts award.

Back Stage at Lincoln Center
http://www.pbs.org/lflc/dec17/sendak.htm
This site from PBS contains an interview with Maurice Sendak about his interest in ballet.

Hillary Rodham Clinton reads **Where the Wild Things Are** *to a group of kids.*

Index